# Brief Notes

# MANAGEMENT OVERVIEW

The publications in *Brief Notes* are outlines of core topics of interest to professionals involved in shopping center management. The outlines are capsule overviews of each topic. Many key points are covered, and shopping center examples are provided for further illustration. Core concepts in each area guide you on topics you may want to explore further. Each outline also contains a helpful glossary.

*Brief Notes* is designed to provide a helpful and informative overview of the topics covered. It is not intended to be a substitute for more extensive learning that can be achieved through attending ICSC educational programs and reading additional ICSC professional publications.

The outlines contained in *Brief Notes: Shopping Center Management:*

- Management Overview
- Finance
- Insurance and Risk Management
- The Lease and Its Language
- Leasing Strategies
- Maintenance
- Marketing
- Retailing
- Security

# Brief Notes

# MANAGEMENT OVERVIEW

International Council of Shopping Centers
New York

## ABOUT THE INTERNATIONAL COUNCIL OF SHOPPING CENTERS

The International Council of Shopping Centers (ICSC) is the trade association of the shopping center industry. Serving the shopping center industry since 1957, ICSC is a not-for-profit organization with over 44,000 members in 77 countries worldwide.

ICSC members include shopping center

- owners
- developers
- managers
- marketing specialists
- leasing agents
- retailers
- researchers
- attorneys
- architects
- contractors
- consultants
- investors
- lenders and brokers
- academics
- public officials

ICSC sponsors more than 200 meetings a year and provides a wide array of services and products for shopping center professionals, including deal making events, conferences, educational programs, accreditation, awards, publications and research data.

For more information about ICSC, write or call the
International Council of Shopping Centers
1221 Avenue of the Americas
New York, NY 10020-1099
Telephone: 646-728-3800
Fax: 212-589-5555
info@icsc.org
http://www.icsc.org

This publication is designed to provide accurate and authoritative information in regard to the subject matter covered. It is sold with the understanding that the publisher is not engaged in rendering legal, accounting, or other professional services. If legal advice or other expert assistance is required, the services of a competent professional person should be sought.

*—From a Declaration of Principles jointly adopted by a Committee of the American Bar Association and a Committee of Publishers.*

Companies, professional groups, clubs and other organizations may qualify for special terms when ordering quantities of more than 20 of this title.

Published by
International Council of Shopping Centers
Publications Department
1221 Avenue of the Americas
New York, NY 10020-1099

ICSC Catalog No.: 242

ISBN: 1-58268-028-0

# Contents

# Preface

Whether a manager is performing the duties of property management or asset management, the shopping center manager's job is to improve the value of shopping center properties and make money for the center's owner. To be successful in today's competitive atmosphere, managers must be aggressive, cost-conscious, creative and, above all else, entrepreneurial.

Successful managers should not only have full knowledge of their properties and market areas, they must possess strong management and leadership skills and, of course, be intimately familiar with the modern tools and resources of the shopping center industry. Achieving this balance will result in improved profitability and the overall success of their centers on both a short-term and a long-term basis.

The material that follows will give you—the shopping center professional—a general understanding of what you must master in order to succeed. Concepts are clearly defined and, for easy reference, a glossary of terms, which will increase a manager's understanding, is included in each section.

Below is a list of resources available through ICSC to help broaden your understanding of shopping center management.

# ICSC RESOURCES

*Books*

- 1,001 Retail Tips and Strategies
- Common Area Maintenance (CAM) Administration
- Crafting Lease Clauses
- CSM Handbook
- Developing a Shopping Center Business Plan
- Effective Newspaper Advertising for Shopping Centers
- Finance for Shopping Center Nonfinancial Professionals
- ICSC's Dictionary of Shopping Center Terms
- Law for Non-Lawyers
- Leasing Small Shopping Centers
- Library of Shopping Center Forms
- Library of Shopping Center Marketing Forms
- Library of Shopping Center Model Letters and Notices
- Library of Small Shopping Center Forms
- Market Research for Shopping Centers
- Marketing Small Shopping Centers
- Operating Small Shopping Centers
- The SCORE
- Shopping Center Lease Administration
- Shopping Center Leasing
- Shopping Center Management
- Shopping Center Marketing
- Shopping Center Redevelopment and Renovation
- Shopping Center Study Lease
- Winning Shopping Center Designs

## Magazines, Reports, Newsletters

- Government Relations Report
- Guide to Writing a Shopping Center Security Manual

- Guide to Writing a Shopping Center Tenant Manual
- Retail Challenge
- Retail Law Strategist
- Shopping Center Legal Update
- Shopping Centers Today

# Acknowledgments

The material in this outline is based in part on a course presented at the International Council of Shopping Centers (ICSC) John T. Riordan School for Professional Development Management Institute.

The International Council of Shopping Centers gratefully acknowledges the individuals mentioned below, who have contributed their expertise to this publication.

John R. Plunkett, SCSM, Shoppers Square
Kurt Sullivan, SCSM

## Core Concepts

✓ Centralized and decentralized operation
✓ REIT

## THE BUSINESS OF OWNERSHIP

Companies that own and/or operate shopping centers have a variety of opportunities available to them to determine how they approach their business models.

- A *centralized system* in which all financial administration is done in the home office—paying all the bills, making the purchases, handling payrolls and all the other financial systems of the company—with only property operations falling under the authority of the on-site manager.
- A *decentralized system* in which almost all aspects of the business are conducted in the field. The system is usually the same for all the centers run by a given company. For

example, all bookkeeping or accounting is done the same way, but it is done by the individual center's management. Each property is its own profit center and is run as a complete business, and each profit center is part of the larger profit center, which is determined by the home office.

- A *hybrid decentralized system.* Although it is a mixture, this system is mostly centralized because the use of computers has tied together many functions. A system may be centralized in its accounting and bookkeeping but still have a decentralized attitude. The manager can still do the buying and approve what is being done while the books are being kept in the home office.

Owners may be REITs, institutions, syndicators or limited partnerships, or individuals. Depending on the type of ownership, goals may vary and can include any combination of the following:

- Long-term stability, with emphasis on value enhancement, preservation of the asset, and strength of the tenant's credit.
- Short-term increase in income and a higher annual return on investment.
- Sale of the center as part of a "Buy-Enhance-Sell" strategy.

Obviously, managers must make it a priority to understand the needs and goals of the owner in order to carry out the requisite management mission.

## Core Concepts

✓ Third-party manager
✓ NOI and FFO
✓ Functions important to successful operation

## THE ROLE OF THE MANAGER

A shopping center manager can be an owner-manager, a manager in the direct employ of the landlord, or a contracted or fee manager, that is, a third-party manager (or management company) that operates the center under contract to the owner.

Shopping center managers are in the business of making money for the owners of their centers and as such should be considered asset managers as well. Their major responsibility is to enhance the value of the asset—the shopping center. In order to carry out this responsibility, managers should be completely familiar with the basics of the operations of their centers—how they physically look and function, how their tenant mix drives business, how their communities perceive their centers and how their property will achieve and maintain future success.

Managers must also be familiar with the basics of the fiscal well-being of their centers—the net operating income (NOI) and funds from operation (FFO). It is their job to minimize expenses and maximize positive cash flow.

## The Qualities of Success

Successful managers have the ability to anticipate, analyze, react to and resolve situations or problems. They focus on what they do, are timely (but wise) in their reactions and remain flexible, shifting gears or directions as necessary. They are friendly in their attitude and enjoy their work—and they regard it as fun. They respect their customers: The tenants, the shoppers and the community in which their center is located.

Good management progresses up what might be thought of as the rungs of a ladder. The bottom rungs are the basics—the physical integrity of the shopping center. The top rung is increased center value. The management ladder includes these rungs:

- Increased value
- Leasing
- Business Planning—Financial and Development
- Budgeting
- Marketing/Community Relations
- Personnel Management
- Crisis Management
- Public relations

- Security
- Maintenance of equipment and physical plant
- Landscaping
- Housekeeping

Managers must understand and pay close attention to the basics of center management—the lower rungs of the ladder—and they must pay attention to them automatically.

## Core Concepts

✓ Cleanliness
✓ Repairs
✓ Preventive maintenance
✓ Inspections
✓ Training of security

## PHYSICAL WELL-BEING OF THE CENTER

Ensuring that a center looks good, is safe, clean and runs efficiently is important to the bottom line. For example:

- A well-maintained center builds sales and can make leasing space easier, which results in fewer vacancies and more productive merchants and reduces operating costs.

### Housekeeping and Landscaping

From the first impression they get when arriving at the center's parking lot to the last impression they take away, shoppers must perceive the shopping center as a pleasant and inviting place. Especially in light of increased competition and the variety of shopping alternatives available to the customer, it is fundamentally important to keep the center clean and attractive. For example:

- Poorly cleaned rest rooms, trash in a parking lot, deteriorating plantings, dirt and litter discourage shoppers from coming to and buying at the stores in the center. Fewer sales mean less income for the center's owners as well as loss of asset value.

## Maintenance of Equipment and Physical Plant

A well-maintained center minimizes operating cost, which has a direct impact on cash flow and profits. For example:

- If you have good rooftop HVAC (heating, ventilation and air-conditioning systems) maintenance, you will lower the chances of having to replace costly components ahead of their natural life expectancy.
- You will be able to anticipate and budget for major repairs, such as a new cooling tower. Reducing the number of unanticipated repairs and service interruptions reduces cost and interference with the tenant's operations.
- Regular preventive maintenance translates into longer useful life of the building and machinery; hence, fewer capital expenditures.
- Constant attention to maintenance of the property reduces hazards and liability claims, ultimately impacting favorably on the center's insurance costs.

To ensure that the highest standards of housekeeping, landscaping and maintenance are being met, successful managers usually schedule regular inspections at varying intervals that are right for their centers. These might include:

- Daily inspections of common areas (such as sidewalks, interior lighting, rest rooms) to ensure that each day the center looks the best it can.
- Weekly inspections of such things as the condition of parking lots and exterior landscaping.
- Quarterly inspections and maintenance checks of such equipment as rooftop units, generators and cooling towers.

## Security and Safety

A shopping center owner must elect whether to supply security services based upon the history of the center and the surrounding community and to what level to provide such service.

Security is usually supplied either by trained employees of the center or by a contracted service.

Well-trained security personnel provide a sense of safety for both shoppers and tenants. A center that is perceived as safe draws and retains shoppers. Additionally, security personnel are in an ideal position to render assistance and information and act as "goodwill ambassadors" since they are often the first to come into contact with shoppers and tenants.

Security personnel may provide the potential for reduction in slips, falls and other hazards by being the "eyes and ears" of the manager on a minute-by-minute basis and addressing issues quickly.

## Core Concepts

✓ Operating statement
✓ Rent reduction or abatement
✓ Default
✓ Evict
✓ Budgets and business plan

## FISCAL WELL-BEING OF THE CENTER

Shopping center managers receive financial reports on a regular basis. Although the names and forms of the various reports may vary, they include a monthly operating statement that details income and expenses. It may include a variance report as well; that is, a report of actual expense or income above or below budgeted projections for that period. This is a key tool for the manager to track progress against plan and provide the owner with revisions, as needed, when circumstances change throughout the year.

### Financial Analysis

Analysis of the monthly operating statement alerts managers to areas that may require immediate action or long-term solutions. It is also a measure of how the center is performing and meeting the owner's goals. Managers should strive to thoroughly understand the information presented in this major management tool. They should know exactly why a number is higher or lower than projected. For example:

- If costs for common area maintenance (CAM)—areas such as parking lots or interior spaces shared in common by the tenants—suddenly rise and exceed the tenants' contributions, those costs will either result in revised, higher tenant expenses or come directly out of the landlord's pocket. Managers must be prepared to deal with such situations, including making prompt and accurate communication to affected parties.

Information on accounts receivable is part of the financial package as well. This report details which tenants are behind in rent and extra charges and how long this has gone on. Managers are ultimately responsible for rent collection, and failure to collect rents in a timely fashion directly affects both cash flow and profitability.

Acting on information contained in the accounts receivable report, managers may be faced with decisions to either help tenants who fall behind or declare them in default (failure to carry out the terms of their leases). For example:

- A manager may decide that a tenant is potentially strong but may need help in the short term to survive. The tenant may be offered a reduction in rent immediately, either forgiving the reduced amount or amending the lease agreement to provide for abatement recovery through rental increases spread over the term of the lease. The final rent may be higher than originally specified in the lease agreement so that the owner will eventually earn back any temporary loss of income.

- Alternately, a manager may decide to evict a defaulting tenant and replace it with a stronger tenant or with one that brings some unique advantage to the center.

## Budgeting

A budget is a financial blueprint or plan. It details what the manager believes will be the actual expenses and income for the center during a given period of time. There is usually a concentration on a twelve-month period, with detailed income and expense figures. Long-term projection of major income and expense numbers (typically for the upcoming three to five years) is a part of financial planning and a business plan.

In constructing a budget it is as wrong to underestimate as it is to overestimate costs or income. This is so because owners must predict their cash flow as precisely as possible for their own financial planning. During the year, adjustments to income and expense allocations may be required. Tenants budgeted to start paying rent on a particular date may be earlier or later than anticipated, or expenses for unexpected repairs may alter the original plan. Communicating a quarterly reforecast of budget projections, therefore, can be an important tool for ownership. Budgets should be developed in detail, with every projected item carefully documented. It is always wise to get the input of others. For example:

- Budget regarding lease-up of vacant space and expiring leases should be assembled by the leasing person.
- Although a marketing director may provide the marketing part of the budget, a shopping center manager must

work with the marketing person to understand and agree with exactly what is being projected.

- If your staff contains personnel to oversee operational areas, such as maintenance and security, the input of these individuals can be quite valuable as well.

## Core Concepts

✓ Minimize, eliminate and transfer risk

✓ Risk management

✓ Insurance coverage

✓ Insurance costs and impact on tenants

## INSURANCE

The purpose of insurance is to share risk. For a fee called a premium, insurance companies agree to assume some portion of the risk of the insured. Insurance is complex. Expert input is useful and many management firms use the services of consultants and brokers who specialize in this critical area of property management. However, even if coverage is purchased centrally by a home office, a manager must understand and analyze all coverages obtained for the property. Typical coverage falls into the following areas:

■ Fire and extended coverage (wind and storm damage, riot, hail, smoke, etc., and the income lost during repairs) against physical damage to a shopping center.

■ Casualty insurance against physical injury or loss claims

(personal injury, false arrest, water damage to tenants' stock, vehicular accident, etc.) from shoppers and other third parties due to activities while at the shopping center.

- Insurance costs are cyclical. For example, the events of September 11, 2001, caused insurance premiums to sky-rocket due to an added emphasis on terrorism insurance and large payouts of claims by insurance and re-insurance companies. The manager needs to be aware of these issues.

It is important for managers to understand proper reporting procedures for insurance purposes: what to say, what to teach staff when filling out report forms, how to deal with the press and the police.

Costs of insurance are generally passed through to tenants. Therefore, it is important to keep costs low and not to allow these costs to escalate substantially from year to year.

## Core Concepts

✓ Crisis management plan
✓ Training and communication with pertinent parties

## CRISIS MANAGEMENT

While we all hope to never have cause to use it, a crisis management plan is essential for each property and the manager is first in line when it comes to developing the plan, communicating it to all parties and implementing it when necessary.

Attending crisis management seminars, reading books on the subject and consulting with local emergency agencies is a way to become familiar with this aspect of management. Then, a formal, written procedure can be implemented detailing specific responsibilities and authorities to be automatically set in motion if a particular crisis should occur.

It is imperative that all staff members partner in the crisis management process, but equally important to brief and educate tenants and local authorities in this regard. Periodic education via memos, training meetings and simulated emergency drills can be effective ways to coordinate the various parties.

Media training is important as a crisis in a shopping center receives the attention of the news media. One spokesperson is usually assigned to this task.

## Core Concepts

✓ Property team
✓ Management style
✓ Key responsibilities

# HUMAN RESOURCES/LEADERSHIP

These are the people who run the center. They are part of a manager's extended family. They are chosen for their expertise, and all of them are part of the team: the marketing director, the assistant manager or director of operations, maintenance staff, landscaping staff, engineers, specialty leasing managers and others, all contribute to a center's bottom line by applying specific expertise that the manager may not possess. The leasing representative, development executive, accountant and others are important members of the team but may or may not report to the center manager.

Usually managers allow department heads the responsibility and authority to, for example:

- Prepare budgets
- Approve expenditures
- Review invoices
- Explain the monthly operating statement
- Deal with day-to-day merchant and shopper issues

When employees believe that what they do makes a difference and feel that management cares, and when they understand the "whys" of things and how their performance is critical to achieving the property's goals, they will be more apt to figure out better ways to do things. This is why leadership plays such a significant role in motivating and inspiring his/her team to actively participate in the success of their property. Management style influences the motivation and performance of team members.

## Core Concepts

✓ Marketing's impact on sales, percentage rent and cash flow

✓ Strategies and tactics

✓ Market definition

✓ Measuring results

✓ Marketing plan

## MARKETING/COMMUNITY RELATIONS

Marketing is vital to the success of any shopping center. It is the "selling" of the product—the shopping center. Marketing for shopping centers builds community relations and tenant sales and helps with leasing.

Everything that relates to marketing can have a very positive impact on sales. Increased sales lead to potential increases in percentage rent and increases in cash flow, and this tells the retailing community that the center is a desirable place in which to do business. (Percentage rent is a negotiated percentage of a tenant's sales that is paid to the center as rent. Minimum rent is the amount of rent that will be paid regardless of a tenant's sales volume.)

Marketing includes much more than holding special events in the center. A sophisticated marketing approach is essential to differentiate the product—the shopping center—from others. To carry this out, centers market their properties using the following strategies and tactics:

- Special events and sales promotions (for example, craft fairs and seasonal sales)
- Advertising (for example, newspaper ads and television commercials)
- Community involvement (for example, mall walking and voter registration drives).
- Public relations (for example, nonpaid exposure in news stories)
- Sponsorships and partnerships (for example, mall walkers program tied in with local hospital)

Marketing planning is based on prior experiences, sound research and available monies.

## Pinpointing the Market

Successful marketing is target marketing. It is an understanding of the trade area and the people in it, so that marketing directors can target their markets accurately. It consists of:

- An accurate definition of the trade area: the geographic area from which shoppers are drawn to the center
- An accurate definition of the demographics within the trade area: the size of the population, the household income, age, sex, marital status, household size, education and ethnic makeup of potential customers
- An accurate knowledge of the psychographics (lifestyles and buying habits) of the people in the trade area

- An accurate knowledge of the media used by the targeted market
- An accurate knowledge of the competition and how it is doing

Demographics change, so in order to be realistic, the market must be reevaluated on a regular basis.

## Quantifying the Results

Every time money is spent in shopping centers for marketing, managers try to see how that expenditure can be measured in terms of results. For example:

- It might draw more people to your center: Traffic counters may indicate an unusual amount of traffic on the day of a special event as compared to a typical day or the same day in the prior year.
- It may show up in actual sales figures: A back-to-school promotion may coincide with a jump in the week's sales figures.
- It may help with leasing.

## Marketing Plan

The marketing plan is a five-step process that begins and ends with research:

1. Situation analysis
2. Problems and opportunity definition
3. Goals and objectives setting
4. Strategies development
5. Tactics planning

# How Managers and Marketing Directors Work Together

A shopping center manager is ultimately responsible for the center and cannot leave marketing solely to the marketing director. Marketing departments located in large centers usually report to the shopping center's general manager. Home office or third-party marketing departments may also report to the manager whether or not based on-site.

## Core Concepts

✓ Partnership with retailers

✓ CRM

✓ Merchant training and motivation

✓ Tenant expectations

## RETAILING

Shopping center managers are, if not literally, at least figuratively, partners with tenants. They must be concerned about sales, how tenants are doing and the entire sales process. Customer service applies not only to the people who come in to buy from the center's retailers but to the manager's own customers—the tenants who make up the shopping center. Customer relationship management (CRM) is a top priority for managers and retailers.

Tenants can be served by providing:

- Direct interaction and personal contact with the tenants by the manager and property management staff.
- Sales seminars, with regular follow-up training

- Opportunities to let weaker tenants benefit from the experience of good merchandisers
- Communications, such as newsletters, meetings, etc.
- Sharing of demographic and other research information obtained by the manager

Managers should know about the business and techniques of retailing. They should take advantage of opportunities to become familiar with retailing terms and practices, the tenants' problems, systems for marking prices up and down, the timing of sales, inventory practices, and training needs. For example:

- A manager should set aside time regularly to talk with the center's tenants including the anchors, such as a big box retailer like a supermarket, a category killer store, and a department store. Department stores are very much like shopping centers, and a manager can learn a great deal about how they operate and apply relevant items to the shopping center.

## What Retail Tenants Expect from Center Management

Tenants expect the following:

- Respect as customers of the landlord
- Clean, safe and appealing facilities
- Enforcement of lease provisions, including center hours, employee parking and signage
- Timely and accurate accounting procedures
- Accurate accounting for common area maintenance, insurance, real estate tax, monitored and controlled marketing expenses and justification for any increases
- Good marketing and sales promotion—for example, an

annual marketing plan that increases traffic and sales and makes for greater public awareness and good community relations

- Good location, design and construction
- Good merchandise mix and leasing plan
- Strong sales results and profits

## What Management Expects of Retail Tenants

Management expects from tenants:

- A strong merchant
- Prompt payment of all lease-required expenses
- An attractive, well-maintained store
- A well-stocked store
- Well-trained and personable salespeople
- Consistent, quality advertising
- Good sales volumes
- Cooperation in issues and matters relating to the common good of the center as a whole
- Active participation in sponsoring events/programs

## Core Concepts

✓ Leasing generates revenue
✓ How the manager helps leasing
✓ Tenant mix
✓ Assembling space

## LEASING

A shopping center's income comes primarily from leasing. Whatever your center's size, it is driven by leasing. A newly leased space within a property results in an increase in cash flow, because it reduces the amount an owner may absorb for such things as CAM and taxes as well as an increase in rental revenue. A vacant space pays no rent and brings in no customers. Leasing provides the tenants who provide the income. The essence of good leasing practice involves:

- Planning ahead—being concerned with placement this year, next year and in the following five years
- Merchandising in a way that relates to trade area desires
- Fair and ethical dealings with merchants and prospects

## Leasing Personnel

Leasing personnel represent the sales end of the shopping center business. They prospect for tenants by visiting other centers, as well as by constantly looking for potentially strong tenants that will fit the desired tenant mix (the variety of different types of retailers and services needed to make an attractive and profitable center).

## The Role of the Shopping Center Manager

Shopping center managers should know what leasing people are doing. Even if they are not officially part of the process, managers are part of the leasing team. Working arrangements may include:

- Having the manager do a major part of the re-leasing, while the leasing representatives do most of the new leasing.
- Making it the manager's responsibility to inform a leasing representative who lives outside the city in which a center is located about what is going on in the center's marketplace.
- Managers should also provide assistance to leasing by showing space to prospects and answering questions about the center, its tenants and overall performance.

Managers have an impact on the lease program when they are knowledgeable about the following:

- The market: the demographics of the trade area
- The center's customers: who they are and what they expect the center to be
- The strengths and weaknesses of the center's tenant mix: For example, if shoe business is down 15 percent, it could

be the economy or the fact that there are too many shoe stores in the center competing unsuccessfully with each other

- Strengths and weaknesses of a competitor's tenant mix
- Trends in merchandising
- Trends in store design and size
- Weak tenants in a center
- Proposed new competitive centers

## Tenant Mix

The center's tenant mix and the relationship of one store to another and to the center as a whole is the most vital part of the leasing process. For example:

- If a leasing representative places a shoe store in Space A, the manager should be aware of how that placement will affect the store that will be leased next door, in Space B, in two or three years.
- If, to improve the mix, a leasing representative has to change the dimensions of a store or combine two store spaces to get a needed larger space, it could mean leaving one space vacant for a while until another becomes vacant and can be combined. This is known as assembling space in the leasing process.
- A well-executed tenant mix of both anchor and small shop stores that meets the needs and desires of the trade area customer is the most essential element to the success of any shopping center.
- The manager should "partner" with his or her leasing personnel to create an overall center "merchandising plan" to develop a long-term vision for the property.

# Core Concepts

✓ Asbestos abatement
✓ Indoor air pollution: mold spores, radon gas, etc.
✓ Underground storage tanks (UST)
✓ Recycling
✓ Hazardous wastes

## ENVIRONMENTAL ISSUES

There is continuous concern with environmental issues. Search the World Wide Web for updated information. Also, trade journals and seminars provide a stream of new information on such subjects as:

- Asbestos and the current law concerning its abatement
- Trends in hazardous wastes
- Inadequate ventilation
- Indoor air pollution, which can result from the use of carbon tetrachloride, benzene and other chemicals used in dry cleaning, and from formaldehyde in carpets and building materials and other chemical contaminants. Cigarette smoke has been virtually eliminated from most buildings

in North America but continues to pose a problem world-wide.

- Mold spores, bacteria, pollen, viruses, and other biological contaminants
- Leaking underground storage tanks (UST)
- Radon

## Recycling

Recycling programs deal with both reality and perception. Environmentally concerned consumers will make some decisions based on your shopping center's concern and participation in these programs. Cost reductions can also be achieved through smart implementation of recycling programs. In many jurisdictions, recycling is mandated by law. Typical items to be recycled include glass containers, newspaper and paper products, corrugated cardboard, chipboard, brown paper bags, tin and aluminum cans, batteries and motor oil.

Additionally, some items such as cleaning fluids, paints, solvents, pesticides, etc. are considered hazardous wastes and must be handled and disposed according to law.

## Core Concepts

✓ Add value, increase NOI
✓ Physical and fiscal responsibilities

# THE ART AND SCIENCE OF MANAGEMENT

The function of shopping center management is to improve the value of the properties involved and to make money for the landlord. To do this successfully, managers need to be knowledgeable about their centers and to use the tools necessary to improve the net operating income and funds from operations of the business. This helps to increase the center's value. A good manager must pay close attention to both the physical (housekeeping and landscaping, equipment maintenance, security and safety) and the fiscal (financial analysis and budgeting) well-being of the center. Further, it's important for managers to understand the specifics of insurance, personnel, marketing, retailing, leasing and environmental issues.

In addition to the skills and tools needed to do the job, the manager must take an entrepreneurial approach to the industry and "make the shopping center his/her own." When true concern for tenants, shoppers and the property itself is displayed, greater efficiency and success become easier to achieve—and the manager will reap an added benefit of being able to perform meaningful and productive work. It is not uncommon to hear a manager refer to the property as "my center" and it is this level of personal concern that sets in place a solid platform on which success for the owner, tenants and shoppers can be achieved.

# Glossary

The glossary that follows lists key definitions compiled from this outline, with several terms not defined in the outline added for your information. The terms are defined within the context of this shopping center management topic.

**Advertising plan**   A description of the message, themes, strategies and creative elements to be used in an advertising campaign.

**Asset management**   An approach that uses all of a shopping center's strengths, both tangible and intangible, in order to achieve the landlord's stated objectives. This approach manages the financial aspect of the center including investments, such as in new leases.

**Balance sheet**   A report showing a business's financial position on a specific date. The report outlines how much the business has, how much it owes and what is left for the stockholders.

**Breakpoint**   The agreed-upon threshhold of a tenant's annual sales in which the tenant is obligated to pay additional overage rent as a percent of sales that exceed that breakpoint.

**Budget**   An itemized listing and/or allotment of all estimated revenues anticipated and a listing (and segregation) of all estimated costs and expenses that will be incurred in obtaining those revenues over a fixed period of time.

**Capital budget**   An outline of expenditures for physical improvements to the property. Tenant improvement allowances intended to provide an incentive to lease space are also considered a capital expenditure. Also known as CAPEX, short for capital expenditure.

**Capital costs**   Money spent on building improvements and tenant improvement allowances. See Capital budget.

**Centralized system**   An administrative system in which all financial systems, including payroll, accounts receivable and payable, purchases, etc., originate from a home office rather than from individual shopping centers. See also Decentralized system; Hybrid decentralized system.

**Certificate of insurance**   A document that is evidence that an insurance policy has been issued.

**Commercial general liability policy**   A broad form of third-party insurance that covers the policyholder in the event of bodily injury, personal injury and property damage.

**Common area maintenance (CAM)**   The process of maintaining a shopping center's common area. Also, a charge that a tenant pays for shared services and facilities such as electricity, security and maintenance in non-tenant space areas of the property.

**CSM**   Certified Shopping Center Manager professional designation provided by the International Council of Shopping Centers.

**Decentralized system**   An administrative system maintained at individual shopping centers (bookkeeping, accounting, purchasing, etc.). Each center is responsible for its work but may follow a standardized system. See also Centralized system; Hybrid decentralized system.

**Default**   The failure to perform on an obligation previously committed. For example, failure to pay rent on a specific date may place a tenant in default of obligations under its lease.

**Demographics**   Basic objective data about shoppers and non-shoppers in a trade area. Includes statistics concerning such things as age, sex, household income, household size, education and occupation.

**Depreciation**   The amount the value of a property deteriorates in a year—how much the total value is reduced by wear and tear.

**Fee manager**   A manager or management firm that contracts to manage a shopping center for a fee or other consideration. A fee manager's relationship with the center's landlord is that of an independent firm hired to render specific services for a specified term of contract.

**Fixed expenses**   Also called indirect expenses, these are operating expenses that are not affected by increases or decreases in sales volume.

**Forecasting**   A budgeting tool used to project both income and expenses through the fiscal end of year. Should be prepared quarterly.

**Hybrid decentralized system**   An administrative system that has the characteristics of both decentralized and centralized administrative systems. It takes advantage of integrated computer systems that tie together such elements as bookkeeping and accounting, but a center manager may do purchasing and approvals although the center's books are kept at a central location. See also Centralized system; Decentralized system.

**Income statement**   A report showing the business's financial performance over a specific period of time. Also known as operating statement and profit-and-loss statement.

**Insurance**   A contract between a risk-taker (the insurer) and another party (the insured) in which, for a fee (the premium), the insurer agrees to pay the insured for losses of something specific (the risk) due to named causes (hazards and perils). The insurer may also assume the obligation to pay a third party (the claimant) on behalf of the insured.

**Letter of intent**   A precontract document stating the terms that the parties are considering prior to the preparation of the lease. Also known as confirmation of business terms.

**Mall mayor**   The merchant who is recognized by peers as an informal leader among the shopping center's tenants.

**Market area**   The area surrounding a shopping center from which the center draws its customers.

**Marketing plan**   A detailed document explaining the five steps and activities a shopping center will use to promote itself during a specific period of time (usually one year).

**Merchandising**  The planning involved in marketing the right merchandise, in the right place, at the right time, in the right quantities and at the right price.

**Merchandise plan**  A long-term strategic plan to add or replace tenants from the center to create "synergy" and maximize shopping opportunities.

**Merchants' association**  An organization of merchants that works to advertise and promote a shopping center. It is a not-for-profit independent corporation.

**Minimum rent**  The base rent a tenant pays; usually expressed as an annual dollar amount or an annual dollar per square foot, regardless of tenant's sales.

**Operating budget**  An outline of how much income a shopping center anticipates and how that income will be spent.

**Operating expenses**  Monies needed to operate a business, as distinct from outlays to finance the business.

**Operating statement**  A management statement that depicts revenue, expenses and net operating income or loss for a fixed period.

**Overage rent**  A form of percentage rent in addition to minimum rent that is derived as a percentage of the tenant's sales that exceed an agreed-upon breakpoint.

**Percentage rent**   Rent the tenant pays; usually based on a percentage of a store's sales.

**Premium**   The fee paid to an insurance company as an inducement for assuming part of the insured's risk.

**Property insurance**   A first-party insurance covering the insured for damages to personal or real property or the loss of its use.

**REIT**   An acronym for a real estate investment trust, a form of ownership of shopping centers and other properties. A business trust or corporation that combines the capital of many investors to acquire or provide financing for real estate. Under U.S. law, a corporation that qualifies for REIT status is not required to pay corporate income tax if it distributes (most) of its taxable income to shareholders.

**Tenant mix**   The types and price levels of retail and service businesses within a shopping center.

**Third-party insurance**   It protects the insured against liability arising out of property or bodily damage to others caused by another party.

**Trade area**   The geographic area from which a center draws its shoppers. Limits that define a trade area may be distance, natural barriers such as rivers or man-made obstructions such as a highway that is difficult to cross.

**Variance report**   Usually part of the financial reporting package provided to (or sometimes prepared by) managers on a periodic basis. It shows an explanation of the difference between budgeted expectations and actual results.